Hey, Are You Listening to Me?

*Listening Your Way to
Professional and Personal Success*

REBECCA A. CARSWELL

REBECCA A. CARSWELL

Originally from New Hampshire, Rebecca moved to Florida to pursue her love of skydiving. In 2002, with over 700 jumps, Rebecca broke her back – she was actually *hit* by the airplane after jumping out of it – 13,500 feet in the air! Despite a negative prognosis and long recuperation, Rebecca recovered completely. She began speaking to organizations about the "Power of Interpretation" – our ability to interpret, or think about, any situation we are in, in any way we choose. In one of Rebecca's most popular presentations, *A Step Beyond the Usual in Communication and Understanding,* she shares her message of communication with businesses, clubs, and organizations, helping people improve their ability to listen, communicate, and understand one another.

Rebecca Carswell is a professional speaker and co-author of *The GROUP: An Amazing Way to Achieve Success, Happiness & Extraordinary Relationships*. She also works with couples and individuals, helping them improve communication skills and achieve goals. She resides on the east coast of Florida with her husband and their four cats.

For contact information or to schedule Rebecca for a speaking engagement at your business, club, or organization, please see the information at the end of this book.

www.RebeccaCarswell.com

To Mike

"The way we communicate with others and with ourselves ultimately determines the quality of our lives."

—Anthony Robbins

CONTENTS

FOREWORD

CHAPTER ONE 1
Why Listen?

CHAPTER TWO 3
Effective Listening: Eight Barriers and Solutions

    #1 Rehearsing 7

    #2 Disagreeing 10

    #3 Telling Your Story 14

    #4 Advising 17

    #5 Assuming 20

    #6 Placating 24

    #7 Judging 27

    #8 Wandering 30

CHAPTER THREE 35
Helpful Tips as You Improve Your Listening Skills

CHAPTER FOUR 37
How to Help People Listen to You

CHAPTER FIVE 41
Who Will Benefit from Better Listening Skills?

CHAPTER SIX 43
Listening in Sales

CHAPTER SEVEN 45
__Listening and Leadership__

CHAPTER EIGHT. 47
__Listening in Business: Problem Solving__

CHAPTER NINE. 51
__Successful Communication__

FOREWORD

Sarah C. Dornin, *Nano Letters*, Harvard University

We live in a new age. The plight of our planet depends on finding solutions to problems, whether environmental or health related, such as disease and starvation. Our future depends on people and countries working together. This requires the ability to communicate with one another. We need to replace broken systems of communication with systems that work.

All of this begins at a very basic level – *with you*. Mahatma Gandhi said that we need to be the change we wish to see in the world. Being able to find solutions and resolve conflicts requires being able to listen effectively, with an open mind. It requires moving past, as Rebecca Carswell calls them, "ego reactions" – the need to be right, the need to win, or to have the last word. And this does not only apply to large companies and world leaders – it applies to each and every one of us. Becoming more effective at communicating and understanding needs to begin with you.

Most of us are never taught how to listen and communicate effectively. And perhaps even more importantly, we are never taught how necessary to our happiness and our relationships this essential skill is.

Indian philosopher Jiddu Krishnamoorthi said that it is only when the mind is quiet and listens completely that there is understanding of truth. Considering, in your mind, possible comebacks before the speaker has finished talking offsets the delicate flow of communication. Even something as simple as taking a defensive stance as you listen shifts the dynamic significantly. Rebecca explores various habits we have of skipping out mentally during a conversation, and how to rectify those habits. She provides for us the means to counter all of the obstacles which prevent us from truly connecting with and understanding another person.

In these pages Rebecca offers effective and easy-to-use tools that will empower your life. I encourage you to seriously consider – *and apply* – what she shares in this book.

Sarah C. Dornin
Assistant Editor, *Nano Letters*
Harvard University
Cambridge, Massachusetts
May 2009

Hey, Are You Listening to Me?

Chapter One

WHY LISTEN?

"To listen well is as powerful a means of communication and influence as to talk well."
—John Marshall,
longest serving Chief Justice of the U.S. in Supreme Court history

Many people think they are already good listeners. The truth is most of us still have a lot to learn when it comes to listening effectively. Ambrose Bierce, an American journalist and satirist who lived in the late 1800's, defined 'conversation' in this way: *"A vocal competition in which the one who is pausing to catch his breath is called the listener."* Many people are simply *waiting* to talk, not truly listening.

So why put the effort into becoming a better listener? Simply put, it makes your life easier and makes you and others around you happier. You are more appreciated by people in your life. Misunderstandings and arguments happen less often. You gain respect from others and come to respect yourself more. Your personal relationships are more fulfilling. Problems are more easily solved. Your professional relationships are stronger – people want to work with those whom they trust, and listening builds trust.

HEY, ARE YOU LISTENING TO ME?

Would you like to...
- Gain respect from employers, employees, and co-workers?
- Increase sales?
- Make your spouse or partner happier (which, of course, means that *you* are happier because when the people around you feel good, you feel good!)
- Boost your child's self-esteem?
- Increase your chances of receiving a raise or promotion?
- Be a better friend?
- Create fewer misunderstandings and arguments?
- Increase teamwork, trust, and cooperation on the job?
- Have people listen to you?
- Reduce stress?
- Connect with others on a deeper level?

What would your life be like with these changes? Easier? More fulfilling? More productive and successful? If you're wondering how you can make these changes, the answer is to become a better and more effective listener.

Good listening skills are *that* important. Developing this essential skill improves your life in every way imaginable.

> *"The most basic of all human needs is the need to understand and be understood. The best way to understand people is to listen to them."*
> —Ralph Nichols,
> head of communication program, University of Minnesota

Chapter Two

EFFECTIVE LISTENING: EIGHT BARRIERS AND SOLUTIONS

"Most of the successful people I've known are the ones who do more listening than talking."
—Bernard M. Baruch,
American economist and past adviser to U.S. Presidents

Being an effective listener is being able to put aside your own agenda and *really hear and understand* what another person is saying. You listen actively to understand the ideas and feelings of the speaker. Listening in this manner is different from the way most people listen – it involves learning how to listen in an entirely new way.

When effective listening is taking place, the listener's mind is open, clear, and quiet. Effective listening occurs when the listener is fully 'present' and listening with his or her *complete* attention. Effective listening can be thought of as listening with your entire body, your entire 'being.' Listening is this way includes the following:

- Listening to *understand*, even if you disagree
- Being alert and open minded
- Asking questions for clarification when needed
- Becoming actively involved and interested in what is being said

- Giving the speaker and what he or she is saying *all* of your focus and attention
- Quieting your mind in order to be fully 'there' for the person speaking

Effective listening is *not*:
- Thinking about what you disagree with
- Letting your mind wander
- Thinking about what you will say next
- Believing that you already know what the speaker is talking about
- Looking for weak points to argue against
- Waiting for the speaker to finish or pause so you can say what you want to say
- Trying to provide answers or advice
- Trying to prove something, such as how your beliefs are more correct or that your point of view is better

With technology and the large amount of multi-tasking we do these days, there are many distractions that keep us from listening effectively. However, the main barrier to effective listening is a busy mind. *Most people's attention is taken up entirely by their own thinking.* The mental noise, or mind chatter, that most of us experience prevents us from being good listeners.

Most people do not realize how much mental noise, or mind chatter, they actually experience at any given moment. Mental noise can 'sound' like this:

Andy, a co-worker, is speaking to you and you start to become bored with what he is saying. Your mind begins to wander. You think about the business dinner you're attending tomorrow evening. Are you prepared for the discussion that will follow the dinner? You make a 'to-do' list in your mind. You tune back in to Andy because he has just said something that you disagree with. You begin to go over, in your mind, the points you will make to correct him. He is always bringing up the same issues, but he never takes any steps towards resolving them. Maybe he just likes to complain. You hope that the business dinner tomorrow night is not a complaint-fest. You happen to notice the hair growing on Andy's ears. He should shave that. This makes you think of a quote. How did that quote go? Something about hair loss as you age being a myth...you don't *lose* the hair, it just relocates – to your ears, your nose, your back. You'll have to look that quote up online when you get back to your desk. You take a moment to interrupt Andy and correct him. He then interrupts you to defend his points. You begin thinking about how he never listens to reason. You wonder how much longer he'll be with the company.

This amount of mental noise happens in our mind in a matter of seconds, and it is happening almost constantly. Despite all the distractions we deal with everyday – both in this fast-paced world in which we live and in our own heads – we *can* improve our listening and communication skills. Taking the time to develop this skill will result in many positive outcomes, both professionally and personally.

In fact, developing your listening skills will improve every area of your life.

In this chapter are eight common barriers to effective listening:
- Rehearsing
- Disagreeing
- Telling Your Story
- Advising
- Assuming
- Placating
- Judging
- Wandering

Also included in this chapter are the solutions to overcoming these eight barriers. As you read, notice how every barrier stems from one thing – a busy, or active, mind. Pay attention to the barriers you observe in yourself most often.

Barrier #1

REHEARSING

Rehearsing is thinking about, or preparing in your mind, what you're going to say before the other person has finished talking. You mentally rehearse important points you want to make or formulate a response to something the speaker said a few minutes ago. You have stopped *effectively* listening, and now you're just *waiting*…waiting for the other person to stop talking, or to pause even, so you can say what you want to say.

You may rehearse when:
- You are trying to impress someone with an intelligent response
- You are eager to make your point
- You want to point out weak points being made by the person speaking
- You feel that your response is important and in order not forget it, you continue to play it over and over in your mind

Solution

Notice that you are rehearsing in your mind. Your awareness is the first step to changing the pattern. Focus solely on what the other person is saying. When you catch yourself thinking about what you want to say, bring your attention back to the speaker. It may seem like you have to refocus your attention often in the beginning, but it will become easier with practice.

When your turn to speak comes, you will know what to say. Your response is *always* better when you really listen than it is when you are rehearsing what to say.

If what you want to say seems so important that you cannot stop thinking about it, write it down. Write down one word that will trigger your memory, then put it out of your mind and return to listening.

Ask Yourself...

When do I *rehearse*? With whom do I *rehearse*?

When you become *aware* that you are rehearsing in your mind, it is easier to begin changing the habit. Take a moment to think about the people you rehearse with while they are speaking. Why do you think you rehearse with these particular people?

Family members/personal relationships:
- Spouse
- Children
- Mother
- Father
- Sibling
- Friend

Work relationships:
- Boss
- Co-worker
- Employee

Other:
- Someone you respect
- Someone you do not respect
- Someone you have recently met

Barrier #2

DISAGREEING

Disagreeing is deciding *before the other person has finished talking* that you do not agree with what is being said. You focus on what you disagree with rather than truly listening and trying to *understand* what is being said. You may listen for weak points – something you can argue against – and feel your rebuttal building inside of you. Rather than effectively listening, you are thinking how *wrong* the other person is! He is *so* wrong, and it's up to you to set him straight and show him the error of his ways. To prove you are right, you may want to promote your own view so badly that you miss the opportunity to explore someone else's view or idea.

When we think that our opinions are the 'truth' – as opposed to simply beliefs – it can prevent us from effectively listening and learning from other's opinions. To experience or witness 'disagreeing,' engage in or watch the following:

- Discussions about religion or politics
- Conversations about global warming
- Political debates between Republicans and Democrats
- Arguments about whose sports team is better

Solution

Human beings have a strong need to be right. We identify on a deep level with our belief systems and viewpoints. Begin noticing this in yourself and in others. (Of course, it's much easier to notice it in others, but more important to notice it in *yourself.*) How do you feel when someone disagrees with your opinion of a movie? What if someone said that your *favorite* movie is long, boring, and consists of terrible actors? What if someone disagrees with your views on politics or religion? Do you call them wrong? Do you stop listening and begin trying to prove that you are right? We all come from different backgrounds, cultures, families, and experiences. We can learn from each other's differences if we choose…or we can try to prove ourselves right and prove others wrong. People in successful relationships know that more will be gained by listening effectively and trying to understand, even if they disagree.

"If there is any one secret of success, it lies in the ability to get the other person's point of view and see things from that person's angle as well as from your own."
— Henry Ford

Keep an open mind. Wait until the other person has finished talking before you decide whether you agree or disagree. Listen to all the points being made. Instead of trying to get across *your* point of view, expressing how your opinion is better or more correct, just listen. When you feel the need to argue your point or prove the other person wrong, bring your focus back to what the other person is saying in an effort to understand.

But why bother listening when you disagree? There are many benefits that can occur when you listen to *understand* someone, despite disagreeing with him or her:

- The other person will be more likely to listen to you.
- You could actually learn something! You may gain some insight into what makes the other person 'tick,' or you may learn something new about the topic at hand.
- When people feel genuinely heard, they usually become less defensive. When you listen in an effort to understand someone, an argument leading nowhere turns into a conversation filled with respect and consideration.
- Less stress! When you listen to understand, as opposed to interjecting and arguing for your beliefs, the conversation is easier and healthier for both parties involved.
- You will have expanded your field of knowledge, even if you do not change your opinion.

You don't always have to *agree* with what the other person is saying, but do your best to *understand* what he or she is saying.

"A good listener tries to understand what the other person is saying. In the end he may disagree sharply, but because he disagrees, he wants to know exactly what it is he is disagreeing with."
— Kenneth A. Wells, author

Ask Yourself...

When do I *disagree*, rather than really listen? With whom do I *disagree*?

Take a moment to make note of the people you disagree with while they are speaking. Notice how the need to prove another wrong interferes with your ability to effectively listen.

Family members/personal relationships:
- Spouse
- Children
- Mother
- Father
- Sibling
- Friend

Work relationships:
- Boss
- Co-worker
- Employee

Other:
- Someone you respect
- Someone you do not respect
- Someone you have recently met

Barrier #3

TELLING YOUR STORY

When someone is sharing a story with you, it may trigger a story or a memory of your own. You decide that now would be a great time to share *your* story! If you are too eager to share your narratives, you may not be allowing the other person to finish, or you may be 'stealing the spotlight' from him or her. Telling your story may sound like this: "Oh yeah…I know *exactly* what you mean! That happened to me about four years ago. I was getting ready to take a trip to see my family…" And you proceed to tell your story.

Telling your story is a common barrier to listening. Most people are more interested in hearing themselves talk than in hearing what others have to say.

Telling your story can also take the form of 'one-upping.' One-upping is trying to 'top' the other person's story with your story. "Oh, that was *nothing*! When I was there last year it was *much* worse…or better…or different…" Or whatever makes your story better in some way. I have heard people 'one-up' with illnesses, surgeries, break-ups, war stories, vacations, childhoods, status, possessions…everything!

This barrier can be seen occurring in a variety of situations:
- Any competitive environment
- With parents and children – "When I was your age…"
- Amongst siblings

- A relationship in which you feel insecure
- A situation in which you feel inferior in some way

Solution

Allow the person speaking to finish his or her story. Ask questions to gain more information. Get involved in what the speaker is sharing. When the other person is finished, if it is appropriate, it may feel natural to share your story. When done correctly and at the right time, sharing stories can be a bonding experience.

It is always a good idea to avoid one-upping. Be aware that the tendency to one-up usually stems from insecurities and wanting to prove that you are better in some way – smarter, richer, stronger and so on. When we one-up in an attempt to make ourselves feel better than someone else, it can momentarily give us an 'ego boost.' After we have one-upped someone, on a superficial and many times unconscious level, we feel 'better' about ourselves for a moment. We feel superior to the person we have just one-upped. This boost to the ego is not real self-esteem – there is nothing positive about it. It is temporary, at someone else's expense, and is born out of insecurity.

If you have a tendency to tell your story or one-up, you may benefit from improving your self-esteem, or working with someone who can help you do this.

Ask Yourself...

When do I *tell my story* or *one-up*? With whom do I *tell my story* or *one-up*?

HEY, ARE YOU LISTENING TO ME?

Take a moment to make note of the people you tell your story to while having a conversation. Are there people you tend to one-up with? Why do you think you need to one-up with these particular people?

Family members/personal relationships:
- Spouse
- Children
- Mother
- Father
- Sibling
- Friend

Work relationships:
- Boss
- Co-worker
- Employee

Other:
- Someone you respect
- Someone you do not respect
- Someone you have recently met

Barrier #4

ADVISING

Advising is listening for how you can 'fix' the problem, rather than truly listening to what is being said. In certain situations or with certain people, you may feel the need to have the right answers. Perhaps you want to impress others with solutions. You are the problem solver, the 'wise one' who knows the answer.

In personal situations, when you care about someone, it can be difficult to see him or her struggling with an issue. You might want to help by telling the person what he should do, what you would do, or what you have done in the past.

Solution

When you notice your mind coming up with solutions or advice that you would like to give, bring your focus back to what the person is saying. Fight the urge to fix the problem or to give advice.

A good rule of thumb is to *ask*, not *tell*. Rather than *telling* the person what to do, *ask* questions for more information. Asking the right kinds of questions is a great way to guide the person to his or her own solution. Examples of questions that can provide clarity or insights are:
- "What are your options?"
- "What is one step you can take to help with this situation?"

- "How are you feeling about this?"
- "What have you done in the past with this kind of problem?"
- "What is one thing you can start doing now to feel better?"

Sometimes the other person may not even be looking for a solution yet. He or she may simply want to sort through or verbalize a recent problem that has arisen. In my private practice I listen in a very active and focused way, with an occasional question for clarification. At times, when my client has finished speaking it is as though a huge weight has been lifted. Many times simply verbalizing a problem – *while someone effectively listens* – can lead to insights and increased clarity.

When someone comes to us with a problem or to 'vent,' we sometimes interpret that as asking for our help, our advice. Why would this person be bringing up the problem if she did not want help solving it? However, unless the other person specifically asks for advice, it is usually best not to give it. Being present and really listening is the best gift you can give another person.

The benefit of listening in this way and questioning in this manner – as opposed to giving advice – goes beyond words. When you guide someone within to find his or her own answers, it is an empowering experience for both parties.

Ask Yourself…

When do I *give advice*? With whom do I *give advice*?

Take a moment to make note of the people you give advice to when they speak to you. Why might you have a need to fix the problem?

Family members/personal relationships:
- Spouse
- Children
- Mother
- Father
- Sibling
- Friend

Work relationships:
- Boss
- Co-worker
- Employee

Other:
- Someone you respect
- Someone you do not respect
- Someone you have recently met

Barrier #5

ASSUMING

We are constantly making assumptions based on our own experiences, belief systems and even our insecurities. We interpret and experience the world around us in our own unique way. Because we do this it can be easy to *assume* that we understand what another person is saying, thinking, or feeling. When we jump to conclusions we often miss what the other person is *truly* saying.

You may feel that you already know what the other person is trying to say. Feeling this way can lead to impatience and you may tune the person out, interrupt, or finish his or her sentences.

Most counselors know that if they *assume* when working with their clients – instead of checking for clarification – they are doing a disservice to the client. The counselor may not have the whole story and may miss important information. Assumptions made with clients, co-workers, friends and family members are the main cause of misunderstandings, arguments, and hurt feelings.

Solution

Try not to make assumptions or jump to the conclusion that you *know* what the other person is thinking or feeling. Listen intently and ask questions for clarification. Reflect back, in your own words, what you believe the person is saying. 'Reflect back in your own words' means to paraphrase or restate what you think the speaker is saying in order to ensure that you do, in fact, understand.

Words can be limiting at times. Using the confines of words to express the wide array of thoughts and concepts in one's mind can be challenging. You have thoughts in your mind and you do your best to convey those thoughts through words. The person listening takes your words in to his mind and *interprets* those words based on *his own* knowledge, experiences, and beliefs. He will probably make his own *assumptions* about what you mean or don't mean. And then he tries to convey his response – based on *his* interpretation of *your* words – back to you through more words...are you confused yet? No wonder communication is so tricky and problematic!

When we stop assuming that we *know* what others are saying, and start to listen to *understand* what they are saying, asking questions when needed, benefits follow:
- Less misunderstandings, arguments, and hurt feelings
- Increased clarity in relationships
- Less time spent fixing problems which originate from assuming
- Fulfilling, trusting relationships
- Acquiring important details or facts relevant to the subject – facts that can be missed when assuming

HEY, ARE YOU LISTENING TO ME?

"I know that you believe you understand what you think I said, but I'm not sure you realize that what you heard is not what I meant."
— Robert McCloskey, author

Ask Yourself…

When do I *assume*? With whom in my life do I *assume*?

Take a moment to make note of the people you assume with while they are speaking. Notice what happens when you assume. Do you finish sentences, interrupt, or simply stop listening? Why do you think you assume with these particular people?

Family members/personal relationships:
- Spouse
- Children
- Mother
- Father
- Sibling
- Friend

Work relationships:
- Boss
- Co-worker
- Employee

Other:
- Someone you respect
- Someone you do not respect
- Someone you have recently met

Barrier #6

PLACATING

Placating is verbally agreeing with everything being said so that it *seems* like you're listening, but really you are only *half* listening. 'Placaters' use phrases such as, "right, right… oh, really…yeah, yeah…uh huh…"

Many books and seminars on listening instruct you to lean in, make eye contact, nod, use placating phrases to show interest, and paraphrase back what was said to show that you understand. Although this makes you *appear* to be listening – which is definitely better than *not* appearing to listen – it may not mean that you actually *are* listening.

That being said, 'acting the part' – leaning in, making good eye contact, nodding – does encourage listening. Communication experts tell us that 90 – 93% of communication is non-verbal. But unless your mental state (a quiet, open, receiving state of mind) is in alignment with your body language, you may simply be acting the part and not actually listening effectively.

When I was in college I received many compliments from classmates regarding my listening skills. Acquaintances would tell me how much they appreciated talking to me because I was a great listener. The truth was, I was a great placater! Although I wasn't a terrible listener, I didn't know how to effectively listen at that time in my life. I thought what I was doing – placating – *was* listening.

Placating can be a common practice when adults are 'listening' to children. It also occurs when we:
- Are preoccupied or have a lot on our mind
- Feel busy and are multi-tasking
- Are on the phone
- Believe we already know what the person is saying (assuming)

Solution

Rather than just *appearing* to listen, actually listen! Don't simply *paraphrase* back what is being said; sincerely check in with the other person to make sure you *understand* what is being said. Use your own words to reflect back what you are hearing. If needed, ask questions for clarification.

Try to refrain from using filler words – "right…uh huh" – and practice intently listening instead. Get involved in what the person is saying.

Ask Yourself…

When do I *placate*? With whom in my life do I *placate*?

Take a moment to make note of the people you placate with while they are speaking. When you placate, are you engaged in another activity at the same time, such as watching television, reading the paper, or working on the computer?

Family members/personal relationships:
- Spouse
- Children
- Mother
- Father
- Sibling
- Friend

Work relationships:
- Boss
- Co-worker
- Employee

Other:
- Someone you respect
- Someone you do not respect
- Someone you have recently met

Barrier #7

JUDGING

Our perceptions of others can cause us to be judgmental at times. People judge others based on age, social status, level of education, sex, race, job title, and many other factors. When we judge someone we may view what he or she has to say as unimportant, and we may not listen.

When we allow judgment to get in the way of really hearing another person, we are closing ourselves off to the human experience. The connections and interactions we have with others – whether those connections last 70 years or 10 minutes – are what make life interesting and fulfilling.

Solution

Judgment happens quickly and many times unconsciously in our minds. How do you feel about people who have more money than you? How about those who have less money than you? Do you experience any judgment towards co-workers who have more prestige than you? How about those who are 'lower' on the corporate ladder? Become aware of prejudices or judgments you have towards others. Awareness of a problem is the first step to changing that problem. Do your best to put preconceived notions aside. Practice seeing each person as you wish to be seen – as valuable, worthy, and having something to contribute.

HEY, ARE YOU LISTENING TO ME?

Everyone wants to be listened to and respected, just as you do. Letting judgment get in the way of listening to someone can close you and the other person off to opportunities. Good managers know that winning ideas can come from anywhere along the corporate ladder. We can learn something from everyone.

> *"The key to success is to get out into the store and listen to what the associates have to say. It's terribly important for everyone to get involved. Our best ideas come from clerks and stock boys."*
> — Sam Walton, founder of Wal-Mart and Sam's Club

Judgment can occur when we feel insecure about ourselves in some way. A feeling of lack or 'not good enough' can cause us to judge others. Often times the people who judge others the most are the ones who judge *themselves* most harshly. Learning self-acceptance and self-love can improve your life, and the lives of those around you, in many ways.

Ask Yourself...

When do I *judge*? With whom in my life do I *judge*?

Take a moment to make note of the people you judge while they are speaking. Realize that when you judge it is an opportunity to look closer at yourself – why might you be judging this particular person? How does it feel when someone judges you?

Family members/personal relationships:
- Spouse
- Children
- Mother
- Father
- Sibling
- Friend

Work relationships:
- Boss
- Co-worker
- Employee

Other:
- Someone you respect
- Someone you do not respect
- Someone you have recently met

Barrier #8

WANDERING

Wandering is when your mind drifts to something happening in your own life while someone is speaking to you. A wandering mind prevents you from listening effectively. You may be thinking about one thing in particular or a plethora of topics – all while the other person is still talking.

A wandering mind is a common barrier and many times happens in conjunction with other barriers to listening. Has this ever happened to you – someone is speaking to you and you start to think about a project due at work next week? Maybe you're making good eye contact with the person, nodding your head, interjecting an occasional "uh huh" or "right" for good measure. But you're actually making a mental list of all the things you need to accomplish to complete that project. Then you suddenly remember that you have to pick up milk and eggs on the way home. Then you begin to fixate on the piece of food stuck in the teeth of the person talking to you. You think, 'Should I tell him about that piece of food?' When your mind wanders in this way, you are not effectively listening.

Solution

When you notice your mind wandering, bring your attention back to what the other person is saying. Be patient with yourself as this takes a certain level of awareness that your mind is wandering in the first place. Continue to bring your focus back as often as needed. With practice, listening effectively will become easier.

If your mind wanders a lot when others are speaking you may need to refocus often in the beginning. The more you practice refocusing in this way, the less your mind will wander. When you practice focusing solely on what another person is saying, you will become better at focusing in other areas of your life. Your mind will become sharper and your concentration will improve.

If there is something you need to remember and you cannot seem to put it out of your mind momentarily for fear of forgetting it, write it down. Then return to listening. If you're worried that you will miss important thoughts by not allowing your mind to wander in this way, keep this in mind: Many psychologists and psychotherapists agree that 90–95% of our thinking is redundant and completely useless.

> *"I think the one lesson I have learned is that there is no substitute for paying attention."*
> — Diane Sawyer, reporter, journalist

Ask Yourself...

When does my mind *wander*? With whom in my life does my mind *wander*?

Take a moment to make note of the people your mind wanders with while they are speaking. What can you do to remind yourself to refocus while you are listening?

Family members/personal relationships:
- Spouse
- Children
- Mother
- Father
- Sibling
- Friend

Work relationships:
- Boss
- Co-worker
- Employee

Other:
- Someone you respect
- Someone you do not respect
- Someone you have recently met

Which of the eight barriers to listening happen to you most often? Is it a combination of barriers that usually happens?
- Rehearsing
- Disagreeing
- Telling Your Story
- Advising
- Assuming
- Placating
- Judging
- Wandering

Be aware of these barriers when you are communicating with others. Awareness of a pattern is the first and many times most important step to changing that pattern. Listening effectively becomes easier and more natural with practice. And the benefits, professionally and personally, are many.

> *"Knowledge speaks, but wisdom listens."*
> — Jimi Hendrix

Chapter Three

HELPFUL TIPS AS YOU IMPROVE YOUR LISTENING SKILLS

Patience

As you improve your listening skills, be patient with yourself. In the beginning listening effectively takes effort, concentration, and determination. You may feel tired after listening intently and effectively – this usually means you are doing it correctly. Listening and focusing will become easier and more natural with practice.

Changing Habits

Whenever we are learning something new or changing an old habit, the process usually gets harder before it becomes easier. Keep with it. Becoming a better listener is worth *every* effort.

> *"Habit is habit and not to be flung out of the window by any man, but rather coaxed downstairs, one step at a time."*
> — Mark Twain

Take one step at a time. Recognize that you are changing an old habit. From the list of eight barriers, identify the main barriers that interfere with your ability to listen well. You may notice two or three that plague you the most or they may all apply to you at one time or another.

Awareness

You must be alert and aware when someone is speaking to you. Notice when your mind becomes active or starts to wander. It's helpful to be able to identify which of the eight barriers is occurring. Sometimes it is a combination of barriers.

Continue to bring your attention and focus back to what the other person is saying. Think of effective listening as 'listening with your whole body.' Put effort into understanding. Actively get involved in what is being said. If needed ask questions for clarification. Reflect back, in your own words, to make sure you understand.

Listen with a Clear, Open Mind

Because we filter what we hear through our own beliefs and experiences – through our own *mind* – it is easy to misinterpret or misunderstand what another person is saying. Imagine your mind being wiped clean – all the judgments, preconceived notions, beliefs, opinions, and agendas put on the back burner. Practice listening with an open and clear mind. Practice *wanting* to hear the message.

Listening, *really listening* is one of the greatest gifts you can give another person. Think about how good you feel when someone allows you to share your thoughts, ideas, or experiences – without judgment. You feel valued, worthy, important. Improving your listening skills benefits the people in your life and it benefits *you*. Keep practicing this important quality and both your professional and personal relationships will improve.

Chapter Four

HOW TO HELP PEOPLE LISTEN TO YOU

If you have a good listener in your life, whether in your personal life or professional life, you are fortunate. It's a wonderful feeling to be able to share thoughts, ideas, and experiences and have someone *really* hear you and be truly interested in what you have to say.

To some people it feels *so* good to have someone listen, that they just keep talking…and talking…*and talking*. These people pose a challenge for effective listeners. Even the *best* listeners can only listen so well and for so long.

Below are three guidelines that will keep good listeners in your life and help you effectively and efficiently share your message.

1. Be concise and clear

Know your message and the point you want to make. When you have the attention of others is not the time to start working out what it is you want to say. It is better to choose your words with awareness, pausing if needed, than to talk continuously in an effort to explain yourself.

When you've made your point, stop talking. It is sometimes helpful to stop talking *before you want to stop*. Many times we have made our point, but will continue trying to support it with extraneous or unnecessary information.

"Many attempts to communicate are nullified by saying too much."
— Robert Greenleaf, founder of the Servant leadership, an approach to leadership development

2. Do not complain

As you may know, things go wrong in life. There are obstacles to overcome. There may be problems in your business, in your relationships, with your health…things will and do go off track. Complaining *never* helps the situation.

When a problem arises, it may be helpful to *evaluate* aspects of the problem, such as: How did it happen? What can you do to prevent it from happening in the future? What can you learn from it? What steps will you take to rectify it? What are your options from this point forward? And so forth.

Complaining does not solve problems – it prolongs them and creates the illusion that they are worse than they really are. For many people, it is difficult and draining to listen to someone who complains.

A favorite author of mine, Eckhart Tolle, says that there are *no problems*…only situations to be dealt with. By being solution oriented, as opposed to complaining, people will want to hear what you have to say.

3. Be aware of any tendency to repeat yourself

You don't need to explain what you are saying in a wide assortment of ways. Once you have made your point, don't repeat your message in a different way just to be sure you are understood. If the person you are speaking to does not understand, he or she will ask for clarification or more information. Or you can ask for feedback. Questions such as, "Am I being clear with what I'm saying?" or "Do you have any questions regarding what I'm saying?" work well to see if your message is being understood. The less time it takes you to express your thoughts, the more your message will be absorbed by those listening.

The above three guidelines pertain more to some situations than to others. In a business or any kind of formal setting, these guidelines should almost always be applied.

In personal, less formal situations, these guidelines may not be necessary all the time. For example, I have had long, exploratory conversations with friends, with repetition and not much concision nor clarity – conversations in which we are sharing our thoughts, exploring feelings, and gaining insights. And I have spent time with friends over pitchers of beer, where everyone is interrupting everyone else, there is 'one-upping' all over the place, and no one is going to stop talking even after he has made his point. There are always exceptions to rules.

Even in the most personal settings, it's beneficial to keep the eight barriers to effective listening in mind and do your best not to complain. These guidelines will always serve you well.

Chapter Five

WHO WILL BENEFIT FROM BETTER LISTENING SKILLS?

Everyone involved will benefit – the person speaking and the person listening. Your co-workers, employees, clients, boss, your children, spouse, friends…you…everyone!

"Listening broadens us…it elevates the quality of our relationships, and opens the way to success. If nothing else, when you listen, you'll find you are the most popular person in the room."
— Linda Eve Diamond, author, speaker

Chapter Six

LISTENING IN SALES

"I only wish I could find an institute that teaches people how to listen. Business people need to listen at least as much as they need to talk. Too many people fail to realize that real communication goes in both directions."
— Lee Iacocca, former CEO Chrysler Corporation

We are all salespeople. We all 'sell' ourselves in some way – our products, our services, our ideas, our beliefs. Successful business people know that *listening* to what their customers need and want, and then giving it to them, is the best way to increase sales and have loyal, happy clients.

I have a friend who for many years sold cars. I don't imagine that this would be the easiest sales job because of how car salespeople are still perceived occasionally by the public. However, my friend was one of the happiest and most successful salesmen I have known. He was incredible at what he did and he loved his job.

His secret? He asked questions and then listened. This sounds simple, but it is extremely powerful. When a potential customer came in, called, or emailed, he asked questions, lots of questions, and then *really listened* to the answers. His mind was not on 'making the sale' but rather on hearing what the person wanted and then doing his best to provide it. By effectively listening to his customers, he made them feel valued, understood, and *heard*. After gathering information regarding what was most important to the customer – for example, safety, gas mileage, price – my friend would make sure he understood: "So, because you and your wife have just had your first child, safety is top priority. You also want something mid-size to accommodate the baby's stroller, changing table, and toys, because you'll be traveling to see family more often now." After he gathered all the information, my friend would proceed to show cars that fit the description of what was wanted. He would site statistics about the safety of the cars he was showing them, and his focus would be on the safety features and on the extra room the car provided. He would help people purchase exactly what they wanted!

His customers were so happy that they referred their friends to him and always returned to him when they were ready to purchase their next vehicle. Asking the right questions – *and then listening* – can give us all the information we need.

The fast-talking salesperson is quickly becoming a thing of the past. People want to work with people who will listen to their needs and solve their problems. To learn about a potential client's needs, you don't talk and tell them what you can do for them. You learn by listening.

People don't respond well when they think others are trying to push something on them without really hearing what they have to say. My friend, the car salesman, created relationships by listening. When potential customers are listened to, their trust in you grows. And people want to do business with those whom they trust.

Chapter Seven

LISTENING AND LEADERSHIP

When your team can talk to you about problems and *you listen to them*, turnover rates decrease. Conflicts are short-lived. Your people are happier and are experiencing greater job satisfaction by being a part of your team. Productivity and quality increase.

Every manager wants to have great listeners on his or her team. Great listeners tend to:

- Be respectful
- Form better relationships with clients
- Work as a team with fellow co-workers
- Create better business to business relationships
- Understand instructions and goals that are being set
- Be solution-oriented

When you are a leader who listens well, you set a strong example for your entire team.

Megan Tough, a business leadership consultant and coach has this to say about listening and leadership: "If there are unhappy or disgruntled people in your business, you can guarantee that at some stage they've tried to tell you what the problem is. It's likely you weren't listening, or didn't want to listen, or perhaps your initial reaction made the person think twice about bringing the problem to you. Truly listening is one of the greatest skills to develop, regardless of your role. Good listeners are genuinely interested, convey empathy and want to find out what's behind the conversation. *Great leaders are great listeners – without exception.*"

When people are heard they feel cared for, valued, and important. Being listened to builds trust and loyalty. A manager who is a good listener creates a strong team.

> *"Of all the skills of leadership, listening is the most valuable – and one of the least understood. Most captains of industry listen only sometimes, and they remain ordinary leaders. But a few, the great ones, never stop listening. That's how they get word before anyone else of unseen problems and opportunities."*
> — Peter Nulty, National Business Hall of Fame, Fortune Magazine

Chapter Eight

LISTENING IN BUSINESS: PROBLEM SOLVING

"No man ever listened himself out of a job."
— Calvin Coolidge, U.S. President (1923-29)

As you know, things go wrong in business. Customers are unhappy, deals fall through, deadlines are not met, conflicts arise between different departments, there is uncertainty about who was responsible for this or that...the list goes on. For some people, when there is a problem, when something goes wrong, there can be a tendency to want to deflect responsibility from oneself. We may look outside ourselves for the cause of the problem. We may want to place blame for fear that *we* will be blamed. We can even become defensive. These kinds of reactions are usually born from the stress of the situation. In times like these we may want to talk – *to explain* – more than we want to listen.

When you find yourself in a problematic situation, feeling upset, maybe even feeling attacked, there are a few guidelines that can help you come out ahead rather than further behind.

Be solution oriented. Keep your eye on the end result – *resolving the problem*. Focus on what can be done from this point forward. Don't let someone's angry or irrational reaction trigger you. Keep breathing – breathing *deeply* helps – and remember to keep your focus on resolving the problem.

Listen, listen, listen. When there is a problem and a customer (or employee, co-worker, family member, friend) is upset, ask questions to find out what happened and then *listen*. Don't interrupt. Be aware of any defensiveness arising in you. Don't make excuses or try to be right. Don't place blame. *Let the other person talk.*

When people are encouraged to talk, they give us information. With this information we can help remedy the problem. The experience of *being listened to* alone can begin to diffuse an upset person.

If it is appropriate, when the person has finished speaking, you can explain the situation and why it happened, from your perspective. If you decide to do this, be very careful. Notice any need in yourself to prove the other person wrong, to make excuses, or to have the last word. Keep it short and clear.

Agreement with the person's *feelings* can further diffuse the situation. When the person has finished talking, try saying, "I can understand why you're upset." Acknowledging the other person's feelings when conflicts arise will increase the chances of a positive outcome. Saying, "I'm sorry" will further increase those chances. If the problem was not something you were directly responsible for, it can be a general apology, such as, "I'm sorry that happened." These simple words go a long way.

When there are problems, a benefit to you and your business will be the ability to put aside 'ego reactions.' Some examples of ego reactions are:

- The need to be right or prove someone wrong
- Making excuses
- The need to belittle or make someone look foolish
- Trying to appear superior
- Wanting to have the last word
- Trying to prove that the customer is being unreasonable
- Not taking responsibility.

The best way to keep an ego reaction from taking over is to recognize it as such and then 'bite your tongue,' breathe, and *listen, listen, listen*. Use the guidelines in this book.

"Let a fool hold his tongue and he will pass for a sage."
— Publilius Syrus, 1st century B.C., *Maxim 914*

And then focus on resolving the problem.

A teacher once asked me, "Do you want to be right or do you want to be happy?" Life becomes easier and more pleasant, and we become more successful, when we decide we would rather be happy. Don't let an ego reaction rob you of happiness and success.

Chapter Nine

SUCCESSFUL COMMUNICATION

Congratulations! With the guidelines contained in this book, you are on your way to becoming a successful and effective communicator. Continue to be aware of the eight barriers to listening and the ones you tend to experience most often. Eventually you will become adept at naming them as they occur. The ability to be aware of the barriers will give you power over them and they will occur less and less.

As your listening skills improve, your family, friends, employees and co-workers will notice the difference, and they will thank you. And because it feels so good to be truly listened to, many of the people in your life will extend to you the same gift.

Be patient with yourself and with your ability to listen effectively in the beginning. Like any skill, it takes time to develop and refine, but *it is worth every effort*. Listening effectively will become easier over time and the benefits you experience will be many.

Thank you for putting the time and effort into becoming a better listener. The world will be a better place with more effective communicators in it. Not only are you improving your own life, you are improving the lives of those around you. You are doing your part to make the world a little better.

> *"The first duty of love is to listen."*
> — Paul Tillich, theologian, philosopher

Rebecca Carswell is a professional speaker, sharing her message of communication with businesses, clubs, and organizations. With her entertaining and eye-opening message, she helps people improve their ability to listen, communicate, and understand one another.

To schedule Rebecca for a speaking engagement, check on her availability, order this book in bulk for a discounted rate, or for general information:
- Visit **www.RebeccaCarswell.com**
- Email **info@rebeccacarswell.com**
- Call **(772) 913-4323**

Rebecca's presentations include:
- *A Step Beyond the Usual in Communication and Understanding*
- *Hey, Are You Listening to Me?*
- *Dealing with Negativity in the Workplace: How to Rise Above It*

Feel free to contact Rebecca with questions or comments.

Made in the USA